Silly Dog Tricks

Fun for You and Your Best Friend

By D. Caroline Coile, Ph.D.
Illustrated by Michael Parker

Sterling Publishing Co., Inc.
New York

Library of Congress Cataloging-in-Publication Data

Coile, D. Caroline.
  Silly dog tricks : fun for you and your best friend / D. Caroline Coile.
      p. cm.
  Includes index.
  ISBN-13: 978-1-4027-1431-3
  ISBN-10: 1-4027-1431-9
  1. Dogs—Training. I. Title.
  SF431.C57 2006
  636.7'0835—dc22

                                              2005034456

10 9 8 7 6 5 4 3 2 1

Published by Sterling Publishing Co., Inc.
387 Park Avenue South, New York, NY 10016
© 2006 by D. Caroline Coile
Illustrations © 2006 by Michael Parker
Distributed in Canada by Sterling Publishing
C/o Canadian Manda Group, 165 Dufferin Street
Toronto, Ontario, Canada M6K 3H6
Distributed in the United Kingdom by GMC Distribution Services
Castle Place, 166 High Street, Lewes, East Sussex, England BN7 1XU
Distributed in Australia by Capricorn Link (Australia) Pty. Ltd.
P.O. Box 704, Windsor, NSW 2756, Australia

Sterling ISBN-13: 978-1-4027-1431-3
        ISBN-10: 1-4027-1431-9

For information about custom editions, special sales, premium and
corporate purchases, please contact Sterling Special Sales
Department at 800-805-5489 or specialsales@sterlingpub.com.

Contents

Tricks Are for Kids—and Dogs!

"Lights! Camera! Action! Speak!" Does your dog have the makings of a Hollywood star? Maybe a circus performer? Magician's assistant? How about the star of his own trick show? Even if your dog's biggest trick is turning your homework into confetti, you can teach him how to put his mind to good use. All you need to teach him some tricks are some instructions and a whole lot of patience!

Teaching your dog tricks is fun! But did you know that it's also important? Dogs that learn tricks are more likely to be well behaved all the time. Learning tricks helps them learn how to learn. That makes it easier for them to learn good manners. Learning tricks takes a lot of brain work and tires dogs out. That makes it harder for them to have the energy to think up lots of trouble to get into! When you teach your dog tricks, you're doing something for your dog that's as important as feeding him—because you're feeding his mind!

Every Trick in the Book

Which trick should you teach first? Here are a couple of hints. First, make sure you read the first chapter, called "Tricks of the Trade." That chapter tells you a lot about how to teach your dog. Once you do that, you can skip around and find tricks you want to try. Your dog should have some say, too—he's the one that's got to do them! He may like to do tricks with his paws, but he may not like to jump. So, pay attention to what he does naturally, and start with tricks that use his natural talents. That's why the tricks are divided into sections according to what your dog needs to do; there are sections on jumping tricks, pawing tricks, speaking tricks, and more.

One more hint: Always read the introduction to each section before you try any of the tricks in it. In some cases, if you teach your dog the very first trick in a section it will make teaching all the other tricks a lot easier!

NOTE TO PARENTS

Teaching the family dog tricks may seem like child's play, but it's one of the most important jobs any family member can undertake. Most families that relinquish their pets to shelters do so either because they aren't attached to them or because the dogs have behavior problems. Getting rid of a family member sends the wrong message to children: that individuals who bore or bother us can be discarded. Trick training not only increases attachment but can alleviate most behavior problems, because lack of human interaction and mental stimulation are the top causes of behavior problems in dogs. Tricks are fun to teach, are low pressure, and give a child a reason to be proud of her dog and herself.

The tricks in this book are designed for healthy dogs with normal temperments. Dogs that are sick or sore should not be pushed to perform tricks that may be difficult or uncomfortable. Fearful or aggressive dogs should be trained by an adult. Trick training can help dogs with some behavior problems, but that training should always be supervised by an adult.

The training methods used in this book probably aren't the ones you learned when you were growing up. They are not new methods, but they are comparatively new to dog trainers. They are kinder and work better than the old-fashioned methods of force training, and they are based on scientific animal-learning principles. If you're not familiar with theses methods, you might just want to read along with your child and find out how you can become a better dog trainer yourself. These methods aren't just for tricks! They work equally well for everyday manners and can be used to treat many behavior problems. They are easy and fun to use and help foster a better elationship with your dog. So, give it a try — prove you can teach an old dog new tricks!

Tricks of the Trade

How do they get dogs in movies to act? How do they get lions in the circus to do tricks? How do they get dolphins in marine shows to do flips? They get the animals to do these tricks by training them using the same methods you can use to teach your dog tricks. They do it by teaching everything in small steps and giving lots of rewards along the way.

Trick and Treat!

When you do something good, you like to be rewarded. The reward might be something you would like to have, such as a dollar or a candy bar. It might be something you'd like to do, such as play a game or go to the movies. Or it might be something that makes you feel good, such as praise or admiration. When you're rewarded for doing something, it makes you want to do it again. Your dog is the same way. The best way to get him to do something is to reward him whenever he does it.

What kind of reward should you use? Just like you, your dog may like lots of different rewards. He probably would like something tasty to eat. You can give him a small dog treat or a tiny piece of meat or cheese. Just make sure the treats are so small that he can't get fat from eating them all! He might also like to play. You can throw a ball for him or let him tug on a toy. Just make sure you don't play so long that he's too tired to finish his lesson! He probably also likes to be petted and praised. You can tell him how smart he is and rub him under the chin. Maybe he would like to go for a walk. Save that for the end of a lesson. Use your imagination and make a list of all of your dog's favorite things—then use all of them as rewards.

What about punishing your dog when he does something wrong? Punishment isn't a good way to teach a dog to do tricks. About the only thing it's good for is to teach a dog to do nothing—and if you want a dog that does nothing, you should get a stuffed toy dog!

It's a Dog's Life

What if you woke up one day in an alien world where dogs ruled? The dogs in charge keep barking at you as if they're trying to tell you something, but you don't know what. They put a collar around your neck. You pick up a toy and they jerk the collar. You touch something else but they jerk you again. They keep barking at you, but everything you do makes them jerk you. Finally you just sit there. You are confused and unhappy. The dogs tell each other, "He sure is dumb. He just sits there."

Now pretend some smarter dogs are in charge. You pick up a toy and nothing happens. You touch a ball and one of the dogs makes a funny noise, like a click, then

hands you a piece of candy. You touch the ball again and the same thing happens. And again! Every time you touch the ball you get that click sound, and every time you hear that click sound you get candy. But now the dog quits giving you the click sound and candy when you touch the ball. Hmmm. You pick it up and instantly you hear *click!* and you get your candy. So now you figure out you have to do more than just touch the ball; you have to pick it up to get rewarded.

But after a while the dog quits rewarding you for picking the ball up. Hmmm. You pick it up and shake it. No click, no candy. You pick it up and throw it in the air—and *click!* Aha! Throwing the ball in the air works! But only for a while. You're catching on, though; it seems that whenever you stop getting the click, the dog just wants you to do something slightly different. All you need to do is try a few things. So you try catching the ball, and sure enough, you hear *click!* and get your reward.

Now the dog finally says something: "Woof." You happened to throw and catch the ball right after he said "Woof," and you got your click and reward. You throw the ball again, before he says anything, and you get nothing. After a few tries you figure out that the only time the dog ever rewards you is when you throw and catch the ball after he says "Woof." Now you wait for him to say "Woof" and you get rewarded!

Now the dog is quiet and you're getting bored. So you try to stand on your head, and suddenly you hear *click!* and the dog gives you a cookie. You try again and do a little better: *Click!* After a while you find out that the dog only makes the clicking sound if you can balance on your head after he says "Arf-Arf."

You wonder what other tricks you can make up that will get rewards. You try all sorts of things, and you get rewarded for lots of them. The dog tells his friends, "He's kind of funny-looking, but he sure is smart. He knows that 'Woof' means to catch and 'Arf-Arf' means to stand on his head! And he's coming up with new tricks all the time!"

Now pretend you're a dog in a world where people rule. Dogs don't understand people rules or language. Punishment only tells them what not to do; it doesn't help

them understand what the right thing to do is. If you were a dog, would you want to be taught by people who used punishment or people who used rewards?

Smart dogs have smart people who know that the best way to teach them is by rewarding them for doing the right things. Whenever your dog doesn't seem to be understanding what you're trying to teach him, remember to put yourself in his place and think like a dog.

The Click Is the Trick

Remember how you couldn't understand what the alien dogs were trying to tell you? They kept woofing and arfing and barking—how were you to know which woofs were meant for you? Your dog feels the same way. You spend all day talking and making people sounds—how can your dog know which ones to pay attention to?

The best way to communicate with your dog when you're training him is to use a sound you don't use any other time. Remember how the alien dogs used a click sound when you did something right? You noticed the click right away because dogs don't normally make click sounds. And it was quick, so you noticed it instantly, as soon as you did the right thing.

You should use the same system when you train your dog. You could say "good" or "that's right" to tell him he's doing what you want, but he's going to have a hard time noticing those words because they sound so much like all those other words you are constantly saying. Plus they take so much longer to say compared to a quick click that, by the time you're through saying them, the dog may be doing something

REMEMBER

1. Click as soon as you can when your dog does what you want.

2. Reward as soon as you can after you click.

3. Don't forget the praise!

else—maybe something you didn't really want to reward! So it's better to use a click sound for a "that's right" signal.

How do you make a click sound? The best way is with a clicker, which is a small, inexpensive object sold at most pet stores. You can also use a noisy ballpoint pen that clicks in and out. Or you can make a click sound with your tongue. It's not quite as good a sound for training, but at least you'll always have it with you!

Does that mean you have to click to your dog forever? No! You click to tell the dog that he has done the right thing only as he is learning each trick. After you are sure he knows the trick, you quit giving him the click. But you still give him praise and rewards!

There's More Than One Way to Train a Dog

Dogs are smart. They can learn tricks lots of different ways. We'll use different ways to train different tricks. If one way doesn't seem to work for your dog, you can try another way. Here are some of the ways to train your dog:

- You can wait for him to do what you want on his own. For example, you could wait for him to bark and then reward him.

- You can place him into position. For example, you might push him into a sit position to show him what you want.

- You can have him use a target to position himself. For example, if you teach him to touch a target with his paw, then you can put the target on other things you want him to paw, such as a light switch.

- You can lure him into position. For example, you might hold a treat in front of him and lead him in a circle so you can teach him to make a circle on his own.

Shape Up!

No matter how you train your dog to do a trick, it won't be perfect at first. It probably won't even look anything like the trick you had in mind! You have to gradually teach him each part of a trick. This is called *shaping his behavior*. Have you ever played the game of Hot and Cold? You hide a prize somewhere and see if another person can find it. When the person goes near the prize, you say, "Warmer!" but if they go away from it, you say, "Colder!" You can't give the person any other clues. As the person follows your cues, she will gradually get closer to the hidden prize. Try it now with someone. . . . Did it work?

Don't let that person leave yet. Try another game with her. Instead of directing her to a hidden prize, direct her to do something you've thought of but haven't told her. And, this time, you can only say "Warmer!"; you can't say "Colder." Let's say you want her to put one hand on top of her head, and you don't feel like waiting for her to do it on her own. So you tell her, "Warmer!" when she lifts her hand closer and closer to her head. You have to watch her carefully because you need to say "Warmer!" as soon as she lifts her hand a little. If you're too slow, she might have already started to put her hand back down by the time you speak, and you'd be saying "Warmer!" when she lowered her hand—just the opposite of what you wanted her to do! But if you are quick and say "Warmer!" right when she has her hand up, she will try it again, and you'll tell her "Warmer!" again. But you really want her to put her hand *on* her head, so next time you wait until she is even warmer, when her hand is a little bit higher. When she tries other positions, you don't say anything. She'll figure out in no time that you want her hand higher, and eventually she'll figure out you want it on top of her head.

Before you try this experiment, remember what we said about how it's easier to give a *click!* sound at just the right instant than it is to say something? So instead of saying "Warmer!" try making a click sound. Pretend

REMEMBER

1. Go in small steps.

2. Perfect each small step before trying to go a step further.

this person can't understand any words you say. Remember: *Click!* = "Warmer!"

But how will this person know that the click means "Warmer!" if you can't tell her? If you give her a prize, such as a penny or a tiny piece of candy, right after each click she will soon learn that a click means she gets a reward. So she'll try to do the right thing to make you click so she can get her reward. You may have to try a few different prizes before you find one this person will work to get. So, now, each time this person gets a little closer to the action you want, you give a click at precisely that moment, and then give her a reward right after the click. Now try it.

Did it work? Congratulations! You're a people trainer! All you need to do now is use a dog instead of a person and you'll be a bona fide dog trainer! Most of the tricks in this book use this method of shaping.

On Cue

Once you've taught your dog that he gets treats for tricks, you need to teach him to do it on cue. Wait until your dog is doing a trick really well. Then add a cue, such as "Speak!" Only click and reward him when he does the trick after the cue; otherwise just ignore him. He'll learn to do the trick when—and only when—you cue him.

One more thing about cues: Half of what makes a dog trick good is a witty cue. Instead of saying "Speak!" to cue your dog to bark, you might say "Be very quiet . . ." because your audience will think it's funny when he barks each time you tell him to be quiet. Thinking of a cue that's the opposite of what your dog will do is one way to make it funny! Be careful, though; your whole family must know what your dog's cues are or they could get upset when the dog does just the opposite of what they ask.

Different Dogs, Different Tricks

Just like people, some dogs are better at some things than others. One dog may like to bark. She will probably be easy to teach tricks involving speaking. Another dog may like to use his front feet to paw at things. He will be easier to teach tricks where he uses his paws. It doesn't mean he can't also learn a barking trick; it just means that it may take him a little longer to learn a barking trick. What does your dog naturally do? Does she bark? Does she paw things? Does she run in circles? Does she jump up on things? Start with a trick that lets her use her natural abilities.

Tricks of the Trade 13

Your First Dog Trick

Before you teach your dog his first trick, you have to teach him what the clicker means. Remember how you gave your person a reward each time you made the click sound? That's what you'll do with your dog. Get lots of little treats ready.

Go *click!* and after about a billionth of a second give him a treat. Do it again and again, click-treat, click-treat, each time giving your dog a treat right after the click. Repeat this about twenty times—maybe twenty more times! Now he is learning that the click is a good thing because it signals that a treat is coming. If he looks at you for his treat as soon as you click, he is a fast learner!

Next, decide what trick to teach him. Or why don't you let him decide? Does he naturally do anything cute? Maybe he stretches and puts his front legs down on the ground with his butt in the air. You could teach him to bow. Maybe he barks. You could teach him to speak. Pick one trick and focus only on it for now.

Let's say he is starting to paw at you because he wants more treats. That could be a trick. You could teach him to put his paw in your lap. As soon as he lifts his paw, click and reward him. Then wait for him to do it again. You may have to wait a while, but be ready. Remember, if you miss it or click too late you will be giving him bad clues. As soon as he lifts his paw, click and reward again. Once he starts lifting his paw a lot, then require him to get it closer to your lap before you click and reward. Once he has the hang of that, require him to touch your lap before clicking. And once he has the hang of that, require him to keep his paw in your lap for a few seconds. Keep requiring him to get "warmer," but only ask for more once he's learned each step. For some dogs that use their paws a lot, this may take only fifteen minutes or so, but for most dogs it may take five or six fifteen-minute training sessions.

Now your dog knows how to put his paw in your lap. But you want him to do it when you ask him to, not just when he feels like it. Only add the cue word (the command) once he knows how to do the trick very well. Then give him the cue ("Are we buddies?") and click and reward him for doing the trick, but don't click or reward him for doing it without the command. You will have to practice each step many (many, many, many, many) times, but in the end your dog will know his first trick!

Letting your dog pick his own tricks by clicking and rewarding him when he does something cute is a fun way to teach him tricks. Some dogs even learn that when you have treats they can try all sorts of new tricks to see if they can come up with one you will reward. But sometimes you want your dog to do a trick that he doesn't naturally do on his own. Now what?

Remember, you can teach almost anything in small steps. Let's say you want your dog to stand with all four feet inside a small box. You could put a box in the room with him and wait for him to step in it, but chances are that would take all day! So, instead you click and reward him for just walking near the box. He'll get the idea that you reward him for walking toward the box, so then you require him to walk even closer to the box before you click and reward. Soon he'll be walking right up to the box. Then you have to ask for more. He will stand there and wait for his click and reward, but it won't come. By now he's figured out that when that happens he has to try something a little different to get you to click. He might try biting the box. No click. Sitting next to the box. No click. Touching the box with his foot. Click and reward! Once he's doing that reliably, don't click until he puts his foot in the box. Then once he's putting one foot in, require him to put two feet in. And the same for foot number three and foot number four!

Of course, you could try a shortcut and just toss some treats in the box so he has to jump in after them. You would still need to click and reward him for getting in, and then you'd gradually use fewer treats to lure him into the box until you weren't using any. Whichever way you use, keep practicing until he knows just what to do to make you click.

Now to make it a trick! Think of a good command; how about "Special delivery!" Click and reward when he gets in the box after you say "Special delivery!" but don't click or reward if you haven't already said it before he gets in. By gradually using a smaller and smaller box, you can teach him to squeeze into a tiny box so it looks like he's trying to mail himself! Congratulations! Your dog knows another trick!

Trick tips

- Teach new tricks in a quiet place away from distractions.

- Don't try to train your dog if he's tired, if he's hot, or if he has just eaten. You want him peppy and hungry for your treats.

- Don't train your dog if you're mad. If you start to get impatient when you are training, it's time to stop.

- Teach your dog with kindness and rewards, not force and punishment.

- Have fun! Learning tricks together should be fun for both of you!

- Always train in gradual steps. Give rewards for getting closer and closer to the final trick. Be patient!

- Give a click instantly when your dog does what you want. The faster you click, the easier it is for your dog to figure out what you like.

- Give a reward as soon as you can after the click.

- Don't forget to praise and pet your dog as part of the reward!

- Don't start using a cue word until you're sure your dog knows the trick.

- Say a cue word just once. Repeating it over and over won't help your dog learn it.

- Once your dog has learned the completed trick and is doing it consistently, you don't have to click your approval any-more. But you still need to tell him he's good and give him a reward.

- Dogs learn better in short sessions. Train your dog for only about ten to fifteen minutes at a time. Always quit while he's still having fun. You can train him several times a day if you want.

- Don't push your dog too fast, and don't let him get too bored. Think of what subjects you like in school. They are probably ones that you are good at but that aren't so easy that they're boring. If your dog tries to run away from training, you're probably making it too hard. If he starts off doing well and then does the same trick worse, you're probably boring him.

- Try to end your training sessions doing something your dog can do well. You want to end on a high note!

- Every step has to be repeated many, many times—we're talking hundreds of times to get it right sometimes! Be patient!

- Remember, your dog didn't read this book! He will have his own way of doing things, and sometimes he will learn faster or slower than the book says. Let him go at his own speed.

- Your dog isn't dumb just because he can't catch on to a trick. If he doesn't seem to get it, try a different trick from another section. If he's smart enough to figure out how to find his food bowl, he's smart enough to learn a trick. You just have to figure out how to talk to him in his own language and make it worth his while.

Ready to get started? You'll need:

- a dog
- a quiet place to practice
- a way to make a click sound
- a reward, such as a toy or lots of little treats

Now pick a trick!

Capture a Dog Trick!

Remember how the alien dog rewarded you if you just happened to do something he liked? He didn't force you to do anything; he just waited for you to do it on your own. That's one way to teach your dog a trick.

Want to try it? Get ready with your clicker and lots of rewards. Think of something cute your dog does or just watch him for a few minutes and pick out something he's doing. Maybe he's just looking at you. When he happens to look at you, click and reward him. Do it again, and again, every time your dog looks at your face. After a bunch of times, is he now looking at you more? If he is, then it's time to add a cue, such as "Pay attention!" Say "Pay attention!" when it seems like your dog might be getting ready to look at you. If he does look at you, click and reward him; if he doesn't, ignore him and try again. If he looks at you when you haven't given him the cue, ignore him then, too. You want him to learn that he gets rewarded only when he looks at your face on cue.

REMEMBER

1. Click and reward an action your dog does naturally.

2. Repeat until he starts doing it over and over.

3. Then add a cue and click and reward only when he does the action on cue.

Teaching dogs to do what they do naturally on cue is called *capturing their behavior.* Dogs that learn tricks this way start figuring out that you will reward them for doing new things, and will often start making up tricks on their own! All the tricks in this first section use this method.

Come

Teaching your dog to come when called
may be the most important trick she can learn.

Your dog probably already comes to you when she wants to play or if you have some food. You want to make sure you reward her for coming to you so she is even more likely to come. When she comes to you when you're in the house, click and give her a reward—give her a treat or play with her for a second. When she comes to you outside, it's even more important to reward her because outside is where she is more likely to get lost or hurt if she doesn't come. Keep clicking and rewarding her so she knows coming to you gets rewarded. Now add a cue, usually the word "Come!" Be sure you click and reward her every time she comes when you call. You don't need to click or reward her when she comes if you haven't called.

PROBLEM SOLVER

What if she comes, but she does it slowly? Here's a way to speed her up: You will need a friend to help you, and a long hallway or other enclosed area. Have your helper hold your dog while you show your dog a yummy treat or favorite toy. Keep showing the reward to her while you back away, so she's pulling and whining to get to it. When she really wants it, call out "Come!" and run away at the same time your friend lets your dog go. When your dog reaches you, click and give her the reward right away. Don't forget the praise! Keep practicing in more open areas as your dog gets the hang of it.

Speak

It's fun to have a talking dog.
If your dog barks at all, you can teach him to bark on cue.

To teach your dog to speak you have to be ready when you think he's going to bark. As soon as he barks, click and reward him. Keep doing this over and over when he barks—try not to miss any barks! Soon he will bark and look at you, expecting his reward. That's when you know it's time to add your cue. Most people use the cue "Speak!"

Say "Speak!" right before it looks like he's going to bark. If he barks, click and reward him. If he barks without you giving the cue, ignore him. After all, your goal isn't to teach him to bark all the time—just on cue! So be very careful to reward him only when he barks after you tell him to.

How can you teach him to whisper?

If you want your dog to whisper, reward him only for barking more and more quietly. Once he's offering quiet barks reliably, then add your cue: "Tell me a secret . . ."

How can you teach him to howl?

It may be harder to teach some dogs to howl since they don't howl as much as they bark. But if your dog howls when you sing or when he hears a siren, you can be ready to click and reward him each time.

How can you teach him to count?

To teach your dog to count by barking, you need to teach him a hand or body signal instead of a voice cue. You can use a hand signal from the start instead of saying "Speak!" or you can add it after you've taught "Speak!" If you add it after, give the hand signal right before you say "Speak!" then gradually say "Speak!" more and more quietly, until your hand signal is much more noticeable. Once your dog barks when you give the hand signal, you need to make your hand signal smaller and smaller, until it's so small nobody in the audience would notice it. Now for the trick! Tell your audience your dog will count or add or subtract or multiply—it doesn't matter as long as you can do the math and the final number isn't too high for your dog to count out in barks. Let's say the answer is "four." You will wiggle your finger to signal your dog to bark once, then wiggle again for another bark, and another, and another, and after the fourth bark you will stop. So should your dog. It will look like he counted to four and stopped!

Doggy Doorbell

Does your dog scratch at the door when he wants to go out? It's natural for dogs to paw at anything, including a door, that stands in their way. But it messes up the door and it's hard for you to hear. Wouldn't it better if your dog had a doorbell? Here's a way to turn your dog's natural behavior into a handy trick.

1. Hang some bells from a strong string, and hang the string from the doorknob on the side of the door where you want your dog to ring the bells. Make sure they hang down low enough so your dog can hit them when he nuzzles or scratches at the door.

2. When your dog tries to scratch the door, he will accidentally ring the bells. Click as soon as he does, then run over and open the door for him.

3. Once your dog gets the idea, you can make the bells shorter so they won't be in your way as much. Only open the door for your dog if he rings the bells without scratching the door.

4. You can leave the bells on the door or move them to a more convenient place if you do it gradually. Continue to let him out only if he rings the bells, and never let him out when he scratches the door.

Warning! Your dog may have so much fun getting you to run to the door that he may drive you crazy ringing the bells!

Kissing Canine

Wouldn't it be nice to have a dog that would give you a kiss when you needed one? Now you can, with just few simple lessons . . . and maybe some tasty treats. If your dog naturally licks your face, you can click and reward her every time she does. Once she's doing it reliably you can add a cue, such as "Nobody loves me," and reward her only for licking on cue. If she doesn't lick your face naturally, you can help her a little bit by doing the following:

1. Get a sticky treat, such as butter or peanut butter, and smear a bit on your cheek.

2. Let your dog lick it off your cheek. Click as soon as she starts licking.

3. Gradually put less and less of the sticky treat on your cheek, but still click when she licks. Hand her a treat when she finishes.

4. You should gradually be able to do away with the sticky goo on your cheek and just click and hand your dog a treat for kissing you.

5. Once she's doing that, add a cue by saying "Nobody loves me . . ." in a sad tone. Click and reward her only when she kisses you after you say that. Soon she will learn that she gets a treat when she kisses you on cue!

PROBLEM SOLVER

What if she won't lick your cheek no matter what? Some dogs just aren't comfortable licking food from people's faces. If yours is one of them, just use the same method to teach her to kiss the back of your hand.

DOGGIE
TREATS

Soccer Dog

Need a teammate who can outrun you? Train your dog to play soccer!

1. If your dog likes to chase balls, roll a soccer ball for him. Make sure the ball is too big for him to pick up. As soon as he touches it with his nose, click and reward him.

2. Once he reliably touches the ball with his nose, roll it shorter and shorter distances, until eventually it's just sitting there. Keep rewarding him for touching it.

3. Now you want your dog to roll the ball. You can wait for him to nudge it on his own, or you can cheat by putting a tiny treat on the ground almost under the ball, so he has to nudge it to get to the treat. Click and reward him when he nudges the ball.

4. Once your dog is nudging the ball to get to the treat, hide the treat under the ball more, so he has to nudge the ball just to see if the treat is there. As soon as he does, click and reward!

5. He should be getting the idea that nudging the ball gets him a reward, so now all you have to do is require him to nudge it a little more and more before rewarding him.

6. Once your dog is pushing the ball with his nose for several feet, add your cue: "Play ball!"

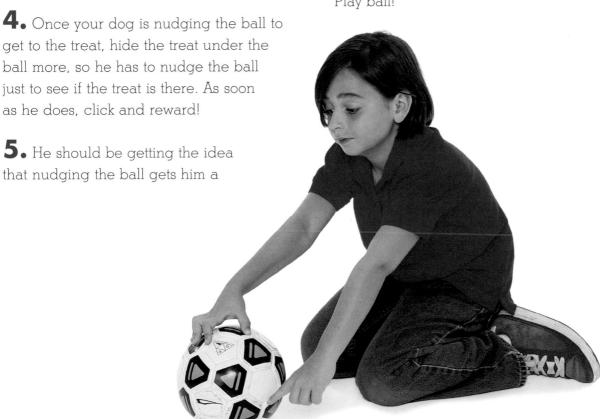

Acrobatics

Dogs with a lot of energy need to exercise their bodies as well as their minds. Why not teach them tricks that do both? Acrobatic tricks include jumping, balancing, and anything athletic. Maybe your dog has a future in the circus!

But not every dog is cut out for these tricks. Some dogs just aren't built to jump or balance. And some may have arthritis or injuries that make these tricks painful. Puppies shouldn't be asked to jump because their joints aren't yet mature, and jumping could injure them. Be sure to check with an adult before trying these tricks. Only practice jumping on grass or carpet—never on slippery floors or hard cement.

Training these tricks mostly means helping your dog discover what she can do. You have to go slowly so you build your dog's confidence. Just as you wouldn't learn to go over a high jump starting at the highest bar, your dog will do better going little by little.

Daredevil Dog

Here's a trick you just might see in a circus! Your dog will jump over some part of you, maybe your leg, your arm—or even your head! But first you have to start by teaching your dog to jump over a stick. Then you'll hold the stick over your leg or arm and gradually take the stick away. Here's how to do it.

1. Get a lightweight stick. A broom handle will work. Balance it between a couple of pillows or bricks so it's a few inches off the ground—even lower if your dog is small.

2. With your dog on a leash, walk over the stick with her, clicking and giving her a treat on the other side.

3. Once she is jumping over the stick eagerly, remove the leash and run beside her, doing everything just as you did when she was on the leash.

4. Once she's jumping reliably off-leash, add the cue: "Ta-dah!" Click and reward her every time she jumps after your cue.

5. Here's the hard step: Have your dog wait while you stand beside the stick until you say "Ta-dah!" Tell her to stay (page 54) or have a friend hold her while you step closer to the stick; then say "Ta-dah!" and let her jump.

6. Once you can stand beside the stick and have your dog jump over it, kneel down and hold the stick a little higher, until it's the height your arm would be if you put your arm alongside the stick while you're kneeling.

7. Hold your arm alongside the stick so your dog is jumping over your arm as well as the stick. Gradually slide the stick closer to your body until she is jumping over just your arm!

8. Do the same thing with your leg. Hold your leg alongside the stick and then gradually let it take the place of the stick. Don't forget to click and treat all along.

9. Now you can gradually raise your arm or leg higher and higher until your dog is really jumping! Be sure you let her jump on only nonslippery surfaces so she doesn't slip or fall.

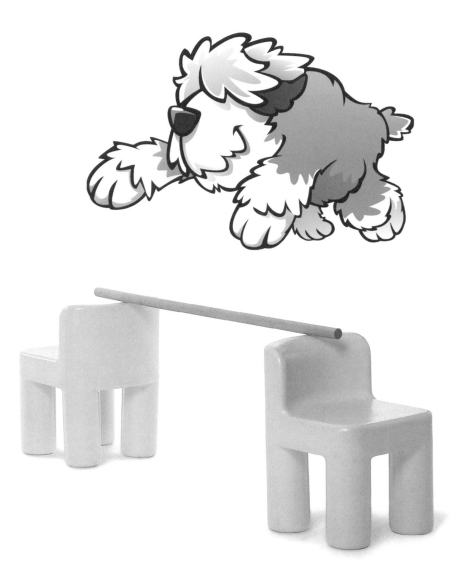

Hoopla Hound

Having your dog jump through a hoop is always a crowd pleaser—and most dogs think it's fun, too! You'll need a hoop. A hula-hoop is ideal, but you can also just tape a small section of rubber hose into a circle. You can put a wire inside the hose so it will keep its shape better. Once you have your hoop, here's how to teach your dog to jump through it.

1. Start by resting the bottom of the hoop on the ground with the dog facing it.

2. Show your dog a treat on the other side of the hoop. You can even reach through the hoop with the treat until it's at your dog's nose. Lure your dog through the hoop by getting him to follow the treat. Once he's on the other side, click and give him the treat.

3. Repeat step 2 until you can just show your dog the treat without having to lead him through the hoop.

4. Raise the hoop a few inches off the ground so he has to jump just a little bit off the ground. Be sure you don't ever make him fall or trip on it, which could scare him and make him quit trying.

5. Once your dog is jumping through the hoop reliably, add your cue: "Ali-hoop!" Click and reward him when he jumps through after your cue.

6. When your dog is jumping on cue, you can raise the hoop a little higher and higher. Eventually you may be able to hold the hoop behind your back and have your dog jump through it.

Open Arms

This trick will work only with small dogs. If your dog is bigger, he might knock you down! But this trick is very cute. When you say "Eek, a mouse!" your dog will jump in your arms and it will look like she was trying to get away from a mouse. Here's how to teach it.

1. Kneel on the floor in front of your dog. Encourage her to run to you and get in your lap. You may need to hold a treat to get her to come. As soon as she is even partway in your lap, click and reward her. Keep practicing, gradually clicking and rewarding her only for getting farther and farther onto your lap, until she is all the way there.

2. Hold your arms down so instead of jumping into your lap she is jumping into your arms on your lap. Click and reward her for doing it right.

3. Now sit up taller and repeat the earlier steps. Gradually require her to get her whole body into your arms before rewarding her.

4. Next sit in a chair so she has to take a small running jump to reach your lap and then your arms. Be sure to click and treat!

5. Once she is jumping up into your arms while you are seated, sit on some cushions on the chair so you can gradually rise up to an almost-standing position without your dog knocking you down. Be sure to catch her! If you drop her she may be too scared to try again.

6. Now stand all the way up and have her leap into your arms!

7. Add your cue: "Eek, a mouse!" Click and reward your dog for jumping into your arms after you cue her.

PROBLEM SOLVER

What if she won't get into your arms even when you're kneeling? You may have to use treats to get her to come into your arms gradually until she feels comfortable there.

What if she is too big for this trick? You can do the trick with just her front paws on your chest or lap.

Beg

Dogs that beg know they can get just about anything they want. So here's your chance to help them. Small dogs usually have an easier time with this trick, but some large dogs can learn, too. Here's one way to teach them.

1. Have your dog sit (see page *50*). Stand behind your dog so your legs are almost touching her back. Reach over the top of her and show her a treat. At first just try to get her to lift her front feet off the ground for a second. Once she gets her teeth on the treat, or gets both front feet off the ground, click and reward her with the treat.

2. Next hold on to the treat a little longer once your dog has grabbed it. Use a dog biscuit or toy so she can hang on to it and steady herself. Because you're standing behind her, if she starts to fall backward you will catch her with your legs. It's very important that she feel secure and not get scared. She will balance better if she is sitting very straight up and down with her paws held close to her body. She will also balance better if her nose is pointing down, so eventually you need to move the treat toward her chest once she gets the idea. Click and reward her for sitting up for just a couple of seconds. Work up to longer times.

3. Gradually change to a smaller treat or toy so she has to depend on it less and less. Click and reward her for balancing by herself for just a second. Gradually work up to longer times.

4. Once your dog is sitting up reliably, add your cue: "Perfect posture!" Click and reward her for sitting up on cue.

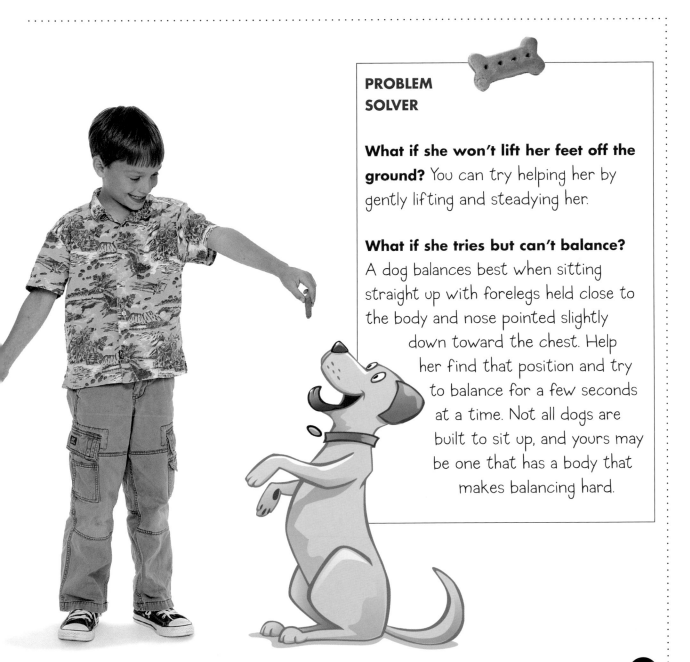

PROBLEM SOLVER

What if she won't lift her feet off the ground? You can try helping her by gently lifting and steadying her.

What if she tries but can't balance? A dog balances best when sitting straight up with forelegs held close to the body and nose pointed slightly down toward the chest. Help her find that position and try to balance for a few seconds at a time. Not all dogs are built to sit up, and yours may be one that has a body that makes balancing hard.

Take a Stroll

Chances are your dog thinks she's a person. So why not teach her to walk like one? Here's how to teach your dog to walk on her hind legs.

1. Stand in front of your dog and show her a treat. Hold the treat up high so she has to stand on her hind legs to get it. As soon as she stands high, click and reward her.

2. After she gets the hang of it, use a dog biscuit or a toy that she can hang on to for a few seconds with her teeth to help her balance. When your dog jumps up to get the treat, hold on to it for few seconds while she holds on to it before you click and give her the treat.

3. Practice having her stand up while holding on for longer and longer times. Then gradually move the biscuit in front of her a few inches. Your dog can either hold on to it or follow it as long as she moves at least one hind foot. Click and reward her as soon as she does.

4. Work on having her go longer and longer without holding on for balance.

5. Gradually get her to take more and more steps. Try to click and reward her before she starts to put her front feet back down. Otherwise she may think you are rewarding her for getting down.

6. Once your dog is walking, add your cue: "Let's stroll!" Click and reward her when she walks on her hind legs when you give the cue.

PROBLEM SOLVER

What if she can't balance? Some dogs aren't built to walk on their hind legs. Still, you can try to help them by steadying them so they are standing straight up with their forelegs close to their body and chin down. If your dog has short legs and a long body, don't even try this trick. It's too hard for them to do and it's bad for their backs.

Simply Fetching

If your dog can fetch, you can do lots of tricks together. Even if your dog loves to play fetch, you still need to teach him how to make it part of a trick. Here's how to teach your dog to fetch reliably.

Throw a ball. If your dog doesn't naturally fetch it, use your clicking and rewarding method to teach her how. First click and reward your dog just for looking at the ball, then going near it, then sniffing it, then taking it from your hand, then holding it in her mouth for a second, then picking it up by herself, then giving it to you, then going to get it, always working gradually to the next step and never going to the next step until your dog has gotten perfect at the previous step. Don't worry; it sounds harder than it is!

Once your dog is fetching a ball reliably, practice retrieving other items, such as gloves, toys, sticks, or items you'll use in your tricks. Keep clicking and rewarding!

You can make a trick out of teaching her to retrieve different items by name. You have to practice each item one at a time and perfect it before adding a cue for it. You can use cute commands for different items. For example, if you want your dog to bring you your cordless phone, you could teach the cue "I hear ringing." Practice fetching the cordless phone over and over, and once she's doing it reliably, add your cue. Only when she is fetching the cordless phone on cue reliably should you teach her the next item. Maybe you want her to bring you a flower; you could use the cue "Who loves me?" Try asking her, "Do you have papers?" and having her bring you the newspaper. Or say "Ah-choo!" to cue her to bring you a box of tissues. Another cute cue is one where you spell the word. For example, you can teach your dog the cue "W-A-L-K" for having her bring you her leash. It will look like she can spell! Just remember—teach each cue one at a time, and only when another cue word is totally learned.

The Amazing Number-Fetching Dog

Does your dog have a nose for trouble? Here's a trick that combines fetching and smelling. Dogs have such a good sense of smell that they can pick out an item you've touched from among a pile of items you haven't. That talent forms the basis of lots of different dog tricks. Here's how to teach your dog to fetch an object with your scent on it.

1. First you need to teach your dog to fetch (see page *40*). For this trick you will need about ten identical items that you can number 1 through 10 (or however many items you have). You could use tennis balls, foam baby blocks, or, for tiny dogs, Ping-Pong balls.
Caution: Don't use anything your dog could inhale or swallow.

2. Pick one item that will have your scent on it. Have an adult tie another item to a big piece of Peg-Board or carpet. Remember not to touch the other item or you will get your scent on it! You may have to use tongs if you want to move the item. Place the Peg-Board or carpet on the ground where you will be training.

3. Rub the item you want your dog to fetch so it has your scent on it. Throw it to one side of the other item, and tell your dog to fetch it. Click and reward her for bringing back the item you threw. If she tries to pick up the other item, she won't be able to because it is tied down. Just ignore her and try again if that happens.

4. Gradually add more items that are tied down. Be sure your scent isn't on them! Throw the scented item gradually closer and closer to the unscented items, until you're throwing it right in the middle of them. Keep clicking and rewarding her for bringing you the right item.

5. For this trick to work best, your dog needs to fetch an item that is just sitting there. So your next step is to teach her to wait a few seconds before letting her run after the item you've thrown. If she starts making mistakes, she's probably been using her eyes instead of her nose to pick out the item that has just landed. So you may have to start by throwing it away from the other items again and doing all the same steps you did before, but make her wait longer and longer before she goes to fetch it. You may have to hold her to keep her from chasing after the item you threw.

6. Gradually place the scented item closer and closer to the unscented ones until you are placing it right in the middle of them. Keep clicking and rewarding your dog for fetching the right item.

7. Now add your cue: "Find!" Click and reward when she brings you the scented item on cue.

8. Next place the scented item in the middle of the other ones, but don't let your dog see you do it! Tell her to "Find!" and click and reward her for doing it.

9. Have somebody else untie all the other items and see if your dog can still find the item with your scent on it. If she can't, retie the other items and train some more.

If she can find the scented item, it's time to go to the next step. Place all the unscented items together in a bag. Remember to use tongs to handle the other items. Hold your scented item to get more of your smell on it and drop it in the bag. Don't leave them together in the bag for long, because your scent will get on the unscented items! A fishnet bag is best because it doesn't trap the scent. Now empty all the items on the

floor and ask your dog to "Find!" She should be able to find your scented item! If she has problems finding it, try using fewer items and working up to more.

10. Now to make it into a trick! Here's one neat trick where you convince your audience your dog can count. Write a number from 1 to 10 on each item. Touch each ball a lot when you do it so they all have the same amount of your scent on them, and then let them all air out for a few days.

Then put them all in the bag. Now tell your audience your dog will pick an item according to its number. Have a member of the audience reach in the bag and pick out any item. This will let the audience know it's a random item.

Take the item from the audience member and make a show of not letting your dog see it, while letting the rest of the audience see it. Although you are pretending to do this so they can see the number, you are really doing it so you can hold the item and get your scent on it.

Place the item back in the bag, then dump all the items out, telling your dog to "Find number two!" or whatever number the chosen item is. The number won't matter because your dog will respond to your "Find" command and pick out the one with your scent—in this case, item number 2!

If you repeat the trick using another number, be sure to put that first item away, not back in the bag with the other items. Otherwise the first item will still have your scent on it, and your dog will be confused if you scented another item.

You can use letters or names or colors on the items; just be sure to let a member of the audience pick it out of the bag and then give it to you.

Pickpocket Pooch

Watch out! This trick could get you in trouble! Your dog is going to steal somebody's wallet right out of his pocket. No, you won't be headed for a life of crime, because you'll need a willing accomplice who will let his pocket be picked. . . .

1. Teach your dog to retrieve an old wallet. Start by throwing it and then gradually making your dog wait longer and longer before letting her get it. Finally just place the wallet down and send her to get it. Be sure to click and treat when she fetches the wallet.

2. Your next step will be easier if you have a helper who will be the one with the wallet in his pocket, but you can do it by yourself if you have to. You want your dog to fetch the wallet from your helper's back pants pocket, so at first have your helper lie down on his belly with the wallet just sitting on top of his pocket. Click and reward your dog for fetching it off your helper's back pocket.

3. Once your dog is doing that step well, place the tip of the wallet in your helper's pocket. Start with just a little bit of the wallet in the pocket, and as your dog gets better at pulling it out, push it slightly farther and farther in. You'll need to leave enough out for your dog to get her mouth around it easily.

4. Next have your friend start to stand gradually, starting by kneeling. If your dog is too short, you may have to teach her to jump on a chair to reach the pocket! Remember to click and treat every time your dog does it right!

5. Now add your cue. You can try something like "I'm broke!" Click and reward your dog only when she fetches the wallet from the pants after you give the cue. When you show this trick to your friends, you will need your accomplice to have his wallet sticking out a little bit and have him stand where your dog can reach it. Your accomplice should pretend he's not in on the trick!

Lead Your Dog by the Nose!

ometimes the easiest way to teach a trick is to tempt your dog into doing what you want by luring him with a treat. For example, let's teach your dog to turn in a circle. You could wait to capture her behavior (see page *18*) by just patiently waiting for her to turn in a circle and then clicking and rewarding her. The problem with that method is that it could take forever!

You could also just take your dog by the collar and spin her in a circle, and then click and reward her. The problem with that method is that it doesn't work very well; to your dog, it seems like what you are rewarding is letting you pull her by the collar. Since she didn't turn voluntarily, it's hard for her to make a connection.

So you need to do something in between these two methods. If you lured your dog into following your treat in a circle, it would be faster than waiting for her to turn by herself, and it would be more voluntary than if you pulled her. This is called *luring your dog*, and it's a very handy way to teach your dog new behaviors.

The hard part about luring is that you have to gradually do away with the lure, or treat, and that can be hard. An easier way is to teach your dog to follow your empty hand or even the end of a stick. Once she knows that, teaching all the other tricks is much easier! Teaching your dog to follow your hand is a neat trick all by itself, so it's the first trick you should learn in this section. It's called Magnet Nose.

You can use the same method to teach your dog to follow the end of a stick. A stick is handier than your hand if your dog is very short, because you don't have to bend down. It's also handy for teaching your dog tricks that have to be done farther away from you.

Note: The instructions for the tricks in this section assume you did not teach the Magnet Nose trick first (even though you should!). If your dog already knows the Magnet Nose trick, just get her to follow your hand instead of a treat in your hand.

Magnet Nose

What if you could lead your dog around by his nose, as though he were connected to your palm by a magnet? You can, and it's easy.

1. Put a treat in one hand, and close your hand to make a fist around it. Let your dog sniff it, and when he touches your hand with his nose, click, open your hand, and let him have the treat.

2. Keep repeating this process, but as your dog gets better, move your hand a few feet so he has to follow it before you give him the treat. Remember to click and treat him when he follows and touches your hand.

3. Once he's good at that, put the treat in your pocket instead of your hand, but show him your hand as usual. When he touches your hand, click and give him the treat from your pocket. Keep repeating this until he gets good at it. If your dog tries to nose the treat in your pocket, ignore him and find a place to keep your treat that is out of his reach.

4. Now gradually open your hand, clicking and rewarding him for touching your palm.

5. Next, practice moving your palm more and more, so your dog has to follow it farther before you click and reward.

6. Now add your cue. Let's use "Magnet on!" When he follows your palm after you say "Magnet on!" click and reward him. This is all your dog needs to know to use this trick to learn other tricks. If you want to make this a neat trick by itself, do the next step.

7. Place a piece of shiny tape on your palm. You can also tape a magnet or anything that looks magnetized to your palm. Tell your audience it is a magnet and that your dog has a voice-activated magnet in his nose. You can prove it because when you turn his magnet on, you can lead him all around by his nose just by moving your hand! Say "Magnet on!" and show them how he is led by his nose by the "magnet" in your hand. When you're finished be sure to say "Turn it off!" and give your dog a big treat.

PROBLEM SOLVER

How would you teach your dog to follow a stick instead of your palm? Use a sticky treat, such as squeeze cheese or peanut butter, that you can plaster on the end of the stick. Then gradually put less of it on the stick and just hand the treat to him after you click for him touching the stick. Do everything else the same way.

Sit

All good dogs should know how to sit. Sitting is part of a lot of tricks, and it's handy around the house. In the old days, everybody taught their dogs to sit by pushing them into position. That method works, but it doesn't work as well as when your dog sits on her own. So instead, lure your dog into a sit. Here's how.

1. When your dog is standing, show her a treat. Move the treat until it's just above her eyes, so she has to tip her nose up to reach it. When she does, click and give her the treat.

2. Keep moving the treat back a little farther so she has to tip her nose back farther to reach it. She will have to bend her knees to reach the treat. If she tries to jump up, gently place your hand on her shoulders to keep her down. Gradually require her to bend her knees more and more before you click and reward her. Eventually she will have to bend her knees so much that she is sitting! Give her a click and a big treat!

3. Next take the food out of your hand. You can use the same hand motion, but give your dog a treat from your pocket instead.

4. When she's sitting to your hand signal, add a word cue: "Sit." Say "Sit" followed by your hand signal, and give your dog a click and reward for sitting. Practice giving just a voice signal or just a hand signal so she will sit to either one.

PROBLEM SOLVER

What if she just backs up? A lot of dogs do that. You can train her on a raised platform or with her rear end next to a wall so she can't back up.

Down

Teaching your dog to lie down is another useful trick, and it's part of such tricks as playing dead and rolling over. It's easier to teach your dog to lie down on a soft raised surface, but you can teach this trick anywhere. Here's how.

1. Start with your dog sitting. Show him a treat and move the treat down to the ground so he follows it with his nose. If he tries to get up, gently hold his rear end down. When he bends his forelegs a little, give him a click and a treat.

2. Gradually require him to lower his legs more and more before you give him the treat. Soon he will be putting his elbows on the floor and lying down!

3. Take the food out of your hand and use just your empty hand to signal him. When he lies down, click and give him a treat from your pocket.

4. Now your dog needs to know when to lie down. Say "Down" and follow your cue with your hand signal. Gradually make your hand signal less noticeable so your dog is responding just to your voice.

5. Once he has mastered lying down from a sitting position, teach your dog to lie down from a standing position. Do it the same way by luring his nose to the ground and gradually rewarding him for getting closer and closer.

STAY

It won't do much good to teach your dog to sit or lie down if he jumps up right away and runs off! He needs to learn to stay in position until you tell him it's okay to move. Staying is a part of many tricks. Just as you did with all the other tricks, you have to start off slowly.

1. Have your dog either sit or lie down. In a soothing voice, say "Stay." If he tries to get up, simply say "Stay," and place him back in position. After a few seconds, say "Okay!" and give him a treat. Then let him get up.

2. Gradually work up to having your dog stay for longer times. Once he's staying for thirty seconds with you standing next to him, tell him to stay and back away from him just a foot or so. If he moves, calmly place him back just as you did before. Wait just a few seconds, return to him, say "Okay!" and give him a treat.

3. Gradually work up to longer times and distances. You don't want your dog to fail, so don't push him too hard or too fast. Sometimes come back after just a few seconds, and sometimes wait longer. Always give him a big reward! Don't go off to play and forget you've left him staying somewhere!

What if he keeps coming to you?
Sometimes dogs come because they are being stared at. When you stare at your dog it makes him feel uncomfortable. In dog language, you're threatening him, and in dog society the way he should cope is to come to you for forgiveness. So don't stare at your dog if you want him to stay!

Dizzy Dog

He spins and spins and where he stops, nobody knows. . . .
The amazing spinning dog dazzles your audience and dizzies your dog.
This trick is easy to teach if your dog knows how to be lured with a stick
or your hand, but you can also teach it using a treat. Here's how.

1. With your dog standing in front of you, show her the treat and move the treat so she follows it in a tight circle. Start by just clicking and rewarding her for turning her head, then for turning just a little bit, then for turning a little bit more until she is turning in a complete circle. Always spin in the same direction.

2. Once your dog is spinning in one circle, try guiding her with just your hand, without holding a treat. When she finishes the circle, click and give her a treat from your pocket.

What about spinning in the other direction? You can teach your dog to spin in the opposite direction the same way you trained her to spin in the first direction. But use a different cue word, such as "Unwind!"

3. Once she spins in one circle to your hand, practice adding on a second circle. Then add another, and another . . .

4. Now it's time to add your cue. How about "Tornado!" Give the cue right before you make the circle with your hand, and click and reward your dog for spinning. If she spins without the cue, just ignore it. Practice until she is reliably spinning when you say "Tornado!"

5. Next you need to phase out using your hand to signal. Make your hand circles smaller and smaller, until your dog is responding to just your voice cue: "Tornado!" Remember to keep clicking and rewarding.

Doggy Detainee

How about a game of cops and robbers? You'll have to be the cop, since your dog can't yell "Freeze!" or frisk you—although that would be a neat trick. You can teach your dog to stop on the word "Freeze!" but for this trick he will learn to "assume the position," as the police say; that is, put his paws against the wall and spread his hind legs so he can be frisked. It helps if your dog already knows how to target with his nose, but it's not necessary.

1. If your dog knows how to target, just stick his target to the wall at around the same height as his head. If he doesn't, plaster some peanut butter on a sticky note and stick it to the wall. Don't stick the food directly to the wall!

2. Encourage your dog to either touch his target on the wall or lick the peanut butter off the paper on the wall. Click and treat as soon as he does either one.

3. Gradually raise the target or food higher on the wall, so eventually he has to put his front feet on the wall to reach it. Be sure to click and reward him every time he touches the target.

PROBLEM SOLVER

What if he just won't put his feet on the wall? Try having him put his feet on a chair, bench, or table. After all, police often have their suspects "assume the position" against the hood of a car.

4. Now that your dog has the basic position, you want to wean him from the treat on the wall if you've been using one. Gradually stick less and less peanut butter to the paper, and finally do away with it and just click and reward when he touches his nose to the target paper looking for his treat.

5. Practice until your dog is reliably touching his target. Then gradually make the target smaller and smaller, until it is altogether gone.

6. Gradually have him stay with his feet on the wall for a little longer before you click and give him a treat.

7. Introduce your cue once he is standing up against the wall reliably. Say "Up against the wall!" and click and reward him when he does so. You may have to remind him using your target paper.

PROBLEM SOLVER

What if he still won't jump up? Dogs with arthritis or back problems may hurt when they try to stretch out and "assume the position." They may do better with another trick.

You can also add "Spread 'em!" but you don't really have to teach him to spread his hind legs, because they will naturally be spread. Just say "Spread 'em!" and it will look like he's obeying you.

8. Finally, get him used to you running your hands down his sides "frisking" him before you click and reward him. Tell him, "Okay; you're free to go," to tell him he can get down.

Roll Out the Barrel!

Here's a circus trick that's easy to teach! It's a little easier if your dog knows the Magnet Nose trick and if she tends to put her front feet on objects, but you can teach it to any dog. If she knows the Magnet Nose trick, you can use just your hand instead of holding a treat right in front of her.

1. You will need a barrel-shaped object that is about the height of your dog's chest. Other than a barrel, a round footstool or trash can might work. Even an oatmeal box might work for a tiny dog. You can also teach your dog to push a baby stroller using the same method. Just have her place her front paws on the handles and use a different command. Put something heavy in the stroller to prevent it from tipping over backward.

2. Lay the barrel on its side. Have your dog face you from the other side of the barrel. Place your foot in front of the barrel so it can't roll.

3. Encourage your dog to place her front feet on the barrel by using either your hand or a treat to lure her. Click and reward her when she puts her front feet on the barrel.

4. Once she's putting both front feet on the barrel confidently, move your foot back just a few inches so the barrel will roll until it hits your foot again. Click and give her a treat before she jumps off!

5. Let your dog get used to the feeling of the barrel rolling, gradually letting it roll a little more each time, making sure she doesn't get scared. It will take her a little while to learn how to move her feet. Hold your hand or treat in front of her and encourage her to go toward it. When she reaches it, click and give her a treat. Walk backward just in front of the barrel so you can urge her toward you and also stop the barrel if it starts rolling too fast. If your dog jumps off or over the barrel, just try again.

6. Once your dog knows what you want and is doing it well and consistently, it's time to introduce her cue word. How about "Steamroller!" Say "Steamroller!" and click and reward your dog for rolling the barrel.

7. When she knows to roll on cue, you can start working on having her roll while you are farther away from the barrel. Stand back from the barrel a few feet and say "Steamroller!" Click and reward your dog for rolling it to you. If she doesn't roll it, stand a little closer and try to move away more gradually. She'll catch on!

Dogcatcher!

Here's a really cute trick: your dog will peer out from between your legs like she's hiding from somebody. Follow these directions to teach it.

1. Go with your dog into a bathroom. Stand in front of the door so you are blocking it with your back to her. Keep your feet slightly apart so the only way out for her is through your legs.

2. Use a treat or your hand (if she knows the Magnet Nose trick) to get your dog to come partway through your legs. When her head sticks through, click and stop her by giving her a treat.

3. Keep repeating this process. Gradually work up to having her stay between your legs for several seconds before you click and treat.

4. Add your cue word. Let's use "Dogcatcher!" Click and reward your dog when she comes to peek out between your legs after you say "Dogcatcher!" Don't reward her for it at other times.

5. You won't look too impressive doing your trick in the bathroom, so you need to work your way to a bigger room once she's doing the trick reliably. Move to a hallway first and practice there. Once your dog is doing the trick in the hallway, move to a larger room. Gradually train her so she can come from anywhere behind you and run to peer from between your legs. Be sure you are still rewarding her!

6. Finally, start standing more naturally with your legs not so far apart. Leave just enough room for your dog to stick her head through—it will look funnier that way!

Crawling Critter

Every canine actor should know how to crawl. It's easier for some dogs than for others, but most dogs can learn. It's easiest to teach if your dog already knows how to lie down and come on command.

1. Place a barrier between your dog and you that is just low enough so he has to crouch down to go under it. You can use a broomstick between two chairs. Have your dog lie down on the other side of the barrier from you. Call or lure your dog to you. As soon as he takes one step in a crouched position, click and give him a treat.

2. Work on having him gradually crawl all the way under the barrier. If he is having problems, you can raise the barrier at first and gradually lower it. Be sure to click and reward him when he is still crawling.

3. Next make the barrier a little longer, so your dog has to crawl for a few more steps.

You could use a second broomstick and drape a sheet over both of them so they make a tunnel. Keep making the tunnel a little longer and longer as your dog masters each distance.

4. Now gradually remove the barrier, starting with any sheet you've draped over it, and then removing each stick, starting from the middle. Eventually you want your dog to crawl the same distance but without

any barriers. Be sure to click and reward while he is still crawling.

5. Once he is crawling reliably, introduce your cue. You could pretend he's a war dog crawling behind enemy lines and shout "Incoming!" Give him this cue before you call him to you. Click and reward him only when he comes after you cue him. Gradually quit calling or luring him and just use the "Incoming!" cue.

Bow Wow Bow

Every performer should know how to bow at the end of a show.

If your dog naturally bows a lot, such as when he wants to play, you can teach him by just waiting for him to bow and then clicking and rewarding him every time he does (see page *18* for more details on capturing a behavior). When he starts bowing and looking at you for his treat, then you add a cue, such as "Take a bow." Once you do that, you click and reward him only when he bows after your cue.

If your dog doesn't bow on his own, you can teach him how. Here's how to do it.

1. With your dog standing, kneel by his side. Take a treat in your hand and put your hand between your dog's front legs from behind, showing him the treat. Your dog should bend his head down to reach the treat. When he does, click and give him the treat.

2. Gradually move the treat back toward his rear, but still between his front legs. Now your dog has to reach between his front legs to get the treat, and that will make him bow a little bit. Be sure to click and reward him as soon as he starts to bow.

3. Keep practicing, gradually moving the treat closer to the ground. Click and reward him for getting his elbows closer and closer to the ground.

4. If your dog moves out of position or tries to lie down, just start over. If he keeps trying to lie all the way down, you can put your other hand under his tummy and guide him so he keeps his rear off the ground.

5. Now, instead of holding the treat in your hand, put it in your pocket and try to get him to bow by just following your hand. When he does, click and reward him with the treat from your pocket.

6. Once your dog is bowing consistently to just your hand signal, add your voice cue: "Take a bow." Then just click and reward him for bowing on cue.

You'll want to practice bowing along with your dog so you look like a team at the end of the show.

Look Smart!

Part of acting is knowing where to look. You can tell human actors what to look at, but how do you tell a canine actor? Hollywood dog trainers have a secret way—and you can teach it to your dog, too! All you have to do is teach your dog to look at a target on cue. Here's how:

1. Use a piece of tape or a little stick-on star—something your dog doesn't see too often. Stick it to a wall or other surface near your dog. If he looks at it on his own, click and reward him. If he doesn't look at it, you can tap on it to get his attention and then click and reward him for looking.

2. Repeat this process until he starts staring at the target more and more and then looking to you for his treat. Then gradually phase out your tapping and pointing.

3. Once your dog is looking at the target reliably, gradually work on having him stare at it longer and longer, maybe for up to thirty seconds.

4. Then add a cue: "Look smart!" Say "Look smart!" and then click and reward your dog for staring at the target. Don't reward him for staring at it unless you've cued him to do so.

Now you can use the target trick to teach your dog all the other tricks in this section.

Mirror, Mirror

"Mirror, mirror on the wall, who's the fairest dog of all?" Why, your dog, of course! And she'll look the part by staring at her reflection in a mirror. Here's how to teach her to do it.

1. Tape a tiny piece of the target she used in the Look Smart! trick (page *67*) to the mirror. Have your dog sit or stand in front of the mirror. Click and reward her for looking at the target.

2. Practice step 1 several times, gradually making her target smaller and smaller. You want it so small that the audience won't notice it. Keep rewarding your dog for looking at the target for longer and longer. Work up to about twenty or thirty seconds.

3. Once your dog is looking at the target reliably, add your cue: ""Who's the fairest one of all? Look smart!" Click and reward her for staring at the mirror after you cue her. Gradually say the "Look smart!" part more and more quietly, and finally quit saying it altogether.

4. A cute addition to this trick is to have her bring the mirror to you (see page *40* for instructions on how to teach her to fetch) or have her run to the mirror. To teach her to run to the mirror, start with her standing farther and farther away from the mirror. Give her the cue ("Who's the fairest one of all?") and click and reward her for approaching the mirror and staring. You should eventually be able to have her start from across the room.

Staring Contest

Dogs that stare at you can be funny. If your dog knows the Look Smart! trick, you can stick her target to just about anything—or anybody—and have her stare at it. You can even stick it to your own face so it looks like she's staring you in the eye. The only problem with this method is that you will look weird with a target stuck to your face! So you need to gradually make the target smaller and smaller, until it's pretty much gone. Here's how.

1. Stick your target to your forehead. When your dog stares at it, click and reward her.

2. Gradually make the size of the target smaller and smaller. Keep clicking and rewarding your dog for staring. When she's just staring at a tiny speck of target, remove it altogether and click and reward her for staring at the same place on your forehead.

3. Keep practicing, requiring her to stare for a few seconds longer each time before rewarding her.

4. Once she's staring at your forehead, add your cue: "It's not polite to stare." Click and reward your dog for staring after you give the cue.

Dog Safety Note: Did you know that not only is it not polite to stare, but it can be dangerous to stare at a strange dog? Dogs stare at one another when they want to say they are the boss. If you stare a dog in the eyes, it can scare the dog because he might think you are threatening him. Or it might make him mad. So don't stare strange dogs in the eye. When you are training your dog, don't stare him in the eye because you may make him feel uneasy.

Yes or No

Should every trick dog know how to nod? Yes! Is it hard to teach your dog to shake his head? No! Every trick dog should know how to nod yes and shake his head no. Fortunately, these tricks are not too hard to teach.

1. Have your dog face you. If your dog already knows the Look Smart! trick, you can stick her target to your hand. Otherwise you can just hold a treat.

2. To teach your dog to shake her head no, move your hand back and forth so she has to move her head back and forth to follow it. When she does, click and treat.

3. Keep practicing step 2. If you are using a treat, gradually do away with it in your hand so your hand is empty. Click and reward your dog with a treat from your pocket.

4. Gradually fade your hand movements so you are moving your hand only slightly. Work on making sure she still moves her head back and forth as if saying no by rewarding only head movements that go beyond your hand movements. If you can get your hand movements small enough, you can also use them as a second, secret hand signal for your dog.

5. When your dog is shaking her head no, introduce a cue, such as "Don't you agree?" Practice using the cue and clicking and rewarding her only when she shakes her head no in response to it.

PROBLEM SOLVER

What about nodding yes?
How would you teach your dog to follow a stick instead of your palm? Don't start teaching your dog to nod yes until she knows how to shake her head no. Then teach your dog using the same technique, except instead of moving your hand back and forth, move it up and down so your dog nods. Once your dog is nodding to your slight hand movements, add a cue such as "Isn't that so?"

Pawsitively Fun Stuff!

Your dog can do lots of tricks using his paws. He can shake hands, give you a high five, play patty-cake, turn off a light, or do just about anything you can think of involve touching his paws to something. He can even cover his eyes! If you teach him to touch his paw to a target and then move the target to what you want him to touch for the trick, it's easy to teach lots of different tricks. So teach your dog the Paw Targeting trick first, then teach him the other tricks in this section. Of course, if you just want to teach him one touching trick, you can go right to that trick.

Some dogs are more likely to use their paws than others. If your dog paws at you to get your attention or uses his feet to reach for things, he's probably a natural for these tricks!

Paw Targeting

One way to teach paw tricks is to teach your dog to touch a target with his paw first. It makes learning all the other paw tricks even easier. Here's what you do.

1. Get a target, such as a sticky note or a piece of tape. If you have taught your dog the Magnet Nose trick, make sure you use a different type of target so he knows which one to touch with his paw and which one to touch with his nose.

2. Let your dog see you place a dog treat under the target. Now place the target where he can't reach it with his nose, but has to paw at it instead. You could place it under a chair, for instance. As soon as he tries to paw the target, even if he doesn't reach it, click and give him a treat from your pocket.

3. Each time your dog gets his paw closer to the target, click and reward him. Once he is reaching for the target reliably, remove the treat from beneath the target so he is just reaching for the target without a treat beneath the target. Click and reward him again for getting his paw closer and closer to the target.

4. Gradually move the target so your dog doesn't have to reach under the chair to get to it. (If he tries to nose the target, he won't get anything, because the treat is no longer under it.) Click and reward him for pawing it.

5. Move the target to slightly different places. Click and reward your dog for touching it with his paw.

6. Now add a cue. How about "Touch!" Say "Touch!" and click and reward if he touches the target. Don't click or reward any other time. Eventually your dog will learn that he gets a reward when he touches the target with his paw after you say "Touch."

7. Now you can gradually move the target away from your dog, so he has to step forward to reach it. Keep clicking and rewarding him when he touches the target. Work up to placing the target across the room, on a chair, or even stuck to a wall.

Can you see how knowing this trick will help you teach your dog other tricks faster? If you want to teach your dog to put his paw in your lap, you could start by putting the target in your lap. Let's use the Paw Targeting trick to teach your dog some other tricks!

Shake Hands

Every polite dog should know how to shake hands.
Fortunately, it's an easy trick to teach.

1. Have your dog sit. Kneel facing him.

2. Reach for his right paw with your right hand. If your dog has already learned to target with his paw, you can use a piece of tape and have him touch it. If he doesn't know how to target, he may naturally give you his paw. If not, you can use a treat to lure his head way to the left, so he's almost looking over his shoulder. His right paw will come off the ground when he does. However he picks his paw up, click and reward him as soon as he does!

3. Keep repeating this process. Click and reward your dog for lifting his paw closer and closer to your hand. If you are luring his head to the side, wait until he is lifting his paw reliably before using only your hand without a treat to lure him. Then gradually lure him less and less, rewarding him only when he lifts his paw.

4. Only when he is lifting his paw and placing it in your hand time after time should you add the cue word. Most people use "Shake!" but since your dog is very polite you may want to use "How do you do?" Give this cue just before it looks like he's going to lift his paw. Click and reward him when he shakes after you give the cue; ignore it when he shakes without the cue. He will soon figure out he gets rewarded only if he shakes on cue!

High-Five Fido

Polite dogs shake your hand. Cool dogs give you a high five. Your cool dog can give a high five by slapping your open palm with his paw. Dogs that like to use their paws to move objects can learn this trick very fast. Here's how to teach it to a dog that already uses his paw. If your dog already knows the Paw Targeting trick, put the target on your palm and start at step 7.

1. Have your dog sit.

2. Kneel in front of him holding a treat in your closed fist on the ground close to his paw.

3. Encourage your dog to get the treat from your hand. As soon as he lifts his paw, click and give him the treat. If he noses your hand, just ignore him and wait for him to make a paw movement.

4. Repeat this, gradually making him move his paw closer to your hand before clicking and rewarding him.

5. Now take the treat out of your hand and just use your empty fist. When he touches your empty fist with his paw, click and give him the treat from your other hand.

6. Gradually open your palm and reward him for touching his paw to your palm.

7. Repeat having him paw your palm, gradually raising your hand higher, clicking and rewarding him for touching your palm with his paw. Finally he should be reaching up to paw your hand.

8. Now to teach your dog when to do it. Let's use the cue "Gimme five!" Say "Gimme five!" just before showing him your palm. Click and reward him for pawing it right away. Now when you say "Gimme five!" your dog will high-five you!

If you've been using the Paw Targeting method, make the target smaller and smaller until it's all gone.

Patty-Cake Puppy

It's easy to teach patty-cake to a dog that already knows the High-Five Fido trick.

1. Teach your dog to touch your palm just as you would in the High-Five Fido trick, but also teach him to touch your other hand with his other paw just the same way. Be sure that you teach him to do just one hand and paw at a time. Only start teaching him to use his other paw when he has mastered using the first one. Only click and reward him when he uses the proper paw.

2. Only when he can do both paws should you start getting him to take turns doing one and then the other. Click and reward each time he uses the correct paw. If he is having problems using both paws, go back and practice each paw separately.

3. As your dog catches on, start to click and reward only after he gets two right in a row. Gradually work up so he has to get three, four, five, or more right, so eventually you can do a whole patty-cake routine. Remember to give him a very big reward for all that work!

4. Add a cue: "Patty-cake time!" before you start the routine. You can also sing the patty-cake song as he does the trick.

Bye-Bye Bowser

It's easiest to teach your dog to wave if he already knows how to do the High-Five Fido trick. The main difference is that instead of touching your palm, he will hold his paw up and follow your palm as you move it up and down out of his reach. Here's how.

1. Teach your dog the High-Five Fido trick, as well as how to sit and stay.

2. Have him sit and stay, and then back away a foot or two from him.

3. Hold your palm up as you would for the High-Five Fido trick. If he lifts his paw, click and reward him before he touches your hand. If he tries to get up, just place him back and start over.

4. Keep practicing with your hand at different heights in front of him. Click and reward him for holding his paw at the same height as your hand.

5. Once your dog is aiming at your hand at different heights, require him to follow it up and down for just a little bit before you click and reward.

6. Keep practicing until he can follow your hand up and down.

7. Now teach him a cue. Say "Wave!" and click and reward him for following your hand. Keep practicing until he is waving only on cue.

8. Next make your hand signal smaller. Do it gradually until it is barely noticeable. Don't forget to click and reward!

PROBLEM SOLVER

What if he won't move his paw up and down? You will have to reward him for moving his paw just the tiniest bit, then gradually reward him for bigger paw movements.

9. Gradually move farther back from your dog so he is waving from a distance. You will have to go to him to reward him.

Lights Out!

Don't you hate it when you get in bed and forget to turn off the light? You can train your dog to do it for you. This is also a cute trick to end a show with. Ask your dog if she's ready for bed, and have her turn off the lights in response. If you have a little dog, you'll have to find a way for her to climb up and reach the switch first. The easiest way to teach this trick is by teaching your dog the Paw Targeting trick (page *77*) first. Then here's what you do.

1. Tape the target to the wall near the light switch. Tell your dog to "Touch" and click and reward her when she does.

2. Gradually move the target so it's right above the light switch. Click and reward your dog for touching it there.

3. Gradually make the target smaller and smaller until it's just a speck. Place it so your dog has to touch the light switch to touch the target. Click and reward her only when she touches the light switch.

4. Once she is reliably touching the light switch, get rid of the target altogether.

5. Next require her not to just touch the light switch, but to pull down on it so it turns the light off. Click and reward!

6. Finally, add the cue: "Ready for bed?" or "Show's over!" Click and reward her only when she turns the light off on cue.

PROBLEM SOLVER

What if she never bumps the switch hard enough? Some companies sell extensions for light switches that make the switches longer so they are easier for dogs (and old people with arthritis!) to move.

What about turning the light back on? It's easier to teach your dog to use her nose instead of her paw to push the switch up. You can do it by using the Magnet Nose method (see page 48) and following the same steps as you used to pull the switch down.

Combination Tricks

Many of the tricks you see canine actors doing have to be taught in their own special way or are a combination of several other tricks. The tricks in this section are those kinds of tricks. But let's learn one more thing before we start.

How do you teach a dog to learn a trick that is a combination of lots of other tricks? You start by teaching each part by itself. Only when your dog knows each part do you start putting them together—but not all at once! Let's say you have a trick where you want your dog to kiss you goodnight, say his prayers, turn out the light, get in bed, and play dead. Wow! First you have to teach him how to do all the different tricks by themselves. Then you start by teaching him how to do the last two tricks together. So you practice having him get in bed and then play dead. You don't click and reward him until he has played dead. You practice this so much it seems like just one trick. Then you add on the trick that comes right before getting into bed, so you would practice having him turn out the light, get in bed, and play dead. Once he is doing this altogether like one trick, you add the trick right before turning out the lights, and so on. You always try to teach the end of a combination trick first. It's easier to remember that way, just like when you sing "The Twelve Days of Christmas" it's easier to remember because you keep adding stuff to the beginning, not the end. Animal trainers call this type of training *back-chaining*.

We will use back-chaining in some of the longer tricks in this section. In some other tricks, we will just try to think of any way we can to get the dog to do what we want!

Wink of an Eye

Want to teach your dog to wink? The winking trick is a little different from most of the tricks in this book because it's based on a different kind of learning called *classical conditioning*. Here's how to do it.

1. Say "Really?"

2. Touch your dog's whiskers on the side his muzzle, on the same side of his face that you want him to wink with.

3. He will automatically blink that eye. Give him a treat.

4. Keep practicing until he starts to wink before you can touch his whiskers.

Now when you say "Really?" to him, he will wink as though you and he were sharing a secret. Get him to nod at the same time (page *74*) and it will be really funny!

What is classical conditioning?
Classical conditioning was discovered by a famous scientist named Pavlov. He accidentally found out that his dogs would drool at the sight of the person who brought them food, whether that person had food or not—just like you may drool at the sight of your favorite drive-through! What happens is that one thing (the drive-through sign) signals that something else (eating a hamburger) will follow it, and eventually you start to react (by drooling) to the sign just as you would to eating the hamburger!

See No Evil

Have you ever seen the dogs on television that cover their eyes when they see something scary? You can teach your dog to do that, too. Here's the secret way the dog trainers teach it.

1. You will need several small pieces of masking tape—not too sticky! Have your dog lie down. Stick a small piece of tape above her eye. She will probably use her foot to try to rub it off. As soon as she gets her foot near her eye, click and reward!

2. You will have to practice this a lot. Keep repeating and then try it by sticking the tape on more and more loosely, and finally with no tape at all. Click and reward for lifting her paw even a little at first.

3. Gradually click only when her foot is closer and closer to her eye, until finally you reward her only if her foot covers her eye.

4. Require your dog to leave her foot in place over her eye for longer and longer, working up to about ten seconds.

5. Now your dog will cover one eye with her foot for several seconds. But you want her to cover both eyes! Start over and train her by putting tape over the opposite eye.

Once you are at the point where she covers the other eye for several seconds, it's time to try for both.

6. Start over and put tape over both eyes. Your dog should reach up with both paws to get it off. If she uses both paws at once, even a little bit, click and reward her. Gradually reward her only for placing both paws over her eyes. Work up to longer times.

7. Once she is covering both eyes, add your cue: "Don't watch!" Click and reward her for covering both eyes on cue.

Once your dog covers her eyes on cue, you can use this trick in a lot of funny ways. She may have to hide her eyes if she sees a scary movie, or if the veterinarian shows her a needle, or if people start kissing near her.

Fire Drill

Stop! Drop! And roll! That's what you're supposed to do if your clothes ever catch fire. Why not teach your dog to do it as well? Then you can practice together. This is a two-part trick consisting of a drop trick and a roll trick.

1. Start by teaching the roll part, which makes a neat trick all by itself. To do that, start with your dog in the down position (page *52*).

2. Next, take your treat, show it to your dog, and move it so she has to twist her head over one shoulder to reach it. When she does, click and give it to her. Once she is turning her head a little, keep moving the treat farther over her back so she has to turn

more. You can help her by gently pushing her over on her side. Click and reward her for turning her head more and more, and especially for rolling onto her side.

3. Once your dog is rolling to one side, keep on moving the treat so she has to roll on her back. Again, you can help her by gently pushing her. Click and reward her for rolling more and more.

4. Continue to move the treat so she rolls onto the opposite side. Continue some more until she is lying back on her stomach. Now just click and reward her for doing a complete roll.

5. Now use your hand without a treat to guide her. When you click and reward her, get the treat from your pocket.

6. Once your dog is rolling on your hand cue, add a voice cue, such as "Fire drill!" Click and reward her for rolling on cue.

7. Once she understands the voice cue, you can phase out the hand cue.

8. Now use the same technique to get your dog to do two rolls in a row. As she finishes the first roll, say "Fire drill!" again and only click and reward when she finishes the second roll. Gradually fade out the second fire drill cue so she is rolling twice when you say "Fire drill!" just once. You can add more and more rolls this way.

9. The parts of this fire drill trick are stop, drop, and roll. So next start from a standing position. Your dog should already know how to lie down on command, so you just have to get her to do it quickly. Say "Fire drill!" and then "Down!" Give her a small treat for dropping to the floor quickly, then another for finishing her roll. Practice this many times, gradually just giving the "Fire drill!" command and only giving the treat at the end of the roll.

10. Once she's dropping from a stand, start having your dog stop while walking and then drop. As she is walking say "Fire drill!" and click and reward her when she stops. Then tell her to drop and roll, giving her a big reward when she finishes.

Play Dead

Your dog needs to do more than just lie there to play dead. To be a convincing actor he will have to drop to the ground, roll on his side, put his head down, and be perfectly still. Most people use the command "Bang!" for this trick, but it's funnier if you say "How's my breath?" so it looks like your bad breath made your dog pass out.

First teach each part of the trick by itself: dropping to the ground, rolling on his side, and being limp.

1. If your dog already knows how to lie down (page *52*), it's easiest to teach him to roll on his side first. Have him lie down as usual. Then lure him onto his side. You can use a treat to lure his head to one side so he shifts his weight to one side, then nudge him over on his side. Click and reward him as soon as he rolls onto his side. Gradually nudge him less and less so that eventually he must roll onto his side without being touched to be rewarded.

2. Once he's lying on his side without being touched, add a cue, such as "On your side."

3. Gradually make your luring less and less obvious. Eventually you want to just give a tiny signal or none at all. Keep rewarding your dog for doing it well.

4. When he knows how to roll onto his side reliably, you can start teaching your dog another part of the trick: being limp. It's easiest to teach it with him already on his side. Start by picking up one foot just barely off the ground and letting it go. If he lets it drop to the ground, click and reward. If he holds it up, just ignore him until he puts it back down. As he learns to relax, gradually pick the foot up higher and higher. Be sure not to pick it up so high it could hurt when you let it go—just a few inches is high enough. You can try to massage him and talk soothingly to him to help him relax. Click and reward him for remaining limp.

5. Teach your dog a cue for being limp. Since this is the last part of your trick, you can teach him the cue for the entire trick. Try using "How's my breath?"

6. Once he can be limp with one foot, move on and do the same thing with his other feet, one at a time. You can also practice having him let you gently touch his chest without him moving, so you can pretend to give him CPR.

7. Once he can be a limp dog, it's time to teach the first part of the trick: dropping into a down position. If he knows the Down command, you just have to practice having him do it from a standing position. You can use a treat to lure his nose down, but eventually you want to reward him only for lying down all the way.

PROBLEM SOLVER

What if he is too excited to play limp? You can skip this part of the trick.

What if he won't quit wagging his tail? Dead dogs wag no tails, but you can just say something like "I see a sign of life" if he does this when you are showing your friends. You can also click and reward him when his tail is still, and gradually teach him not to move it—but that can be hard to teach! (It's easier to teach him to wag his tail—can you figure out how? Hint: use the capturing a behavior method on page *18*.)

8. Once he's dropping to a down from a stand, add a cue: "Drop!"

9. You want your dog to drop to a down position fast, so practice walking and then having him drop quickly. Click and reward him for dropping a little bit faster and faster. If he won't drop fast, don't worry—the trick is still funny whether he "dies" quickly or slowly.

10. Only when your dog knows all three parts of the trick is it time to put them together. He already knows how to be limp, so you want him to know to roll on his side and then be limp when you give him the cue "How's my breath?"

11. When he's lying down, say "How's my breath? Roll!" and gently nudge him to roll. Then pick his paw up to give him the limp dog test. If he's limp, click and reward. Keep repeating this until you can drop the "Roll!" part of the cue.

12. Once your dog will roll on his side and be limp, it's time to add the first part of the trick. When he's standing, say "How's my breath? Drop!" and tell him to drop, then roll, then be limp. Click and reward for doing all three. Keep repeating, and as he gets better, gradually drop the "Drop!" from the cue.

Now when you say "How's my breath?" your dog should drop, roll on his side, and remain limp.

PROBLEM SOLVER

What if he jumps up as soon as you offer his the treat? Many dogs just can't eat on their sides or with their heads down. If yours is one of them, have him stay, then tell him, "Okay," before you give him the treat. You can even use the command "He's alive!" to let him know he can jump up and get his treat. It makes a good finish!

Say Your Prayers

There are lots of ways for your dog to say her prayers. One neat way is to have her sit and place her front paws on the side of a bed or chair and to bow her head between them. This trick takes several steps to train.

1. Start with your dog sitting while facing a bed or chair within paw's length. Let's use a chair.

2. You want to teach her to place her front feet on the edge of the chair. If she knows the Paw Targeting trick, you can place her target on the chair and have her put a paw there. Then work on encouraging her to put her other paw there. You can encourage her by patting the chair or by using a treat. If she naturally waves her paws around, you may be able to hold a treat up just over the chair and she may raise a paw and place it on the chair. If she does, click and reward her! If she doesn't tend to use her paws, just gently place them on the chair and instantly click and reward her. Keep practicing by clicking and rewarding as soon as she puts her paws on the chair.

3. Once your dog is putting her paws up reliably, you want to teach her to bow her head. Hold the treat between her front legs, so she has to look down between her legs to see it. If she moves her paws, just start over. Gradually lure her head down between her legs and then click and give her the treat. Once she is doing this well, remove the treat from your hand. Click and reward her for bowing her head toward your empty hand.

4. Now introduce a cue. It's cute to have a cue that makes it sound like your dog is in trouble and praying for help. You could say "Uh-oh!" or "Prayer time!" Give your dog the cue just before using your hand to lure her into position. Be sure to give her a click and a big reward!

Hang Eight!

How about letting your dog join in your skateboarding adventures? He may not be able to do some of the fancy tricks, but when a dog can skateboard, that's a pretty fancy trick all by itself. Here's how it's done.

1. You will, of course, need a skateboard. You could try to lure your dog on it, or put him on it, but the easiest way is to have him trained to put his paw on a target (page *77*), and then put the target on the skateboard. Hold the skateboard still so it doesn't roll. Click and reward him for placing his paw on the target on the skateboard.

2. Require him to leave his paw on the target for longer and longer times before rewarding him.

3. Once he's leaving his paw on the skateboard for thirty seconds or so, let the skateboard move just a few inches. Click and reward your dog for leaving his paw in place.

4. Now let's add another paw to the board. You want your dog to put his other front paw and his hind paw on the same side on the board. You can wait for him to do it, but it's probably easiest to lure him into climbing up on the board using a treat or your palm (if he knows the Magnet Nose trick). Click and reward him for leaving his paws in place.

5. Now place your treat in front of your dog so you are luring him forward. Let the board move a little, but don't let it get out of control. You want it to move only a couple of inches so it doesn't scare him at first. Click and reward your dog as soon as he stays on the board while it moves. If he tries to get off, just try again.

6. Keep luring him forward. He will have to push with his hind leg that's not on the board. Click and reward him for any progress!

7. Work on having your dog move the board farther and faster. As he gets the hang of it, he may naturally pick his last foot up so he can coast on the board. Be sure to click and reward him as soon as he does.

8. Now to add a cue. What else could it be but "Hang eight!" Click and reward him for pushing the skateboard on cue.

Some dogs really love this trick. You may be able to push the skateboard out and have your dog chase it and jump on it just for the fun of it. Some dogs can even hold the skateboard with their teeth and launch it, then jump on it and ride!

Copycat Dog

Copycat Dog is a neat trick that is really just a lot of other tricks done with hand or body signals. The trick starts by saying "I need a mirror." After that you do several things your dog knows how to do—maybe sit, lie down, roll over, and twirl in a circle. Instead of telling your dog what to do, you will be giving your dog hand signals that the audience won't notice. They will think your dog is copying you. Teaching hand signals is easy. Let's say you want to teach a hand signal for your dog to sit.

1. Teach your dog how to sit (or do any trick) using the voice command as usual. Or just use a hand signal, or both hand and voice signals, from the start!

2. If you are adding a body or hand signal after your dog knows a voice cue, give the hand signal just before you give the voice command. You want to repeat these signals together so often that when your dog sees the hand signal she knows the voice cue is coming, so she eventually just starts to sit to the hand signal.

3. Once your dog is sitting just to your hand signal, gradually make your signal smaller so it is less noticeable to other people.

4. Work on giving her a hand signal and also doing the act you want your dog to copy. So give your dog a signal to sit, then sit yourself, and click and reward your dog for sitting. If you want, you can make your position act as a body signal to your dog, so when you sit down, that's the signal for your dog to sit, for example.

5. Use the same technique to teach her different hand signals for different tricks.

6. Gradually work up to doing more than one trick before giving her a big reward. Start with just two, then three, then four. If you want to do the tricks in the same order every time, be sure to start training with the last trick and work backward toward the first trick.

Now you can say "I need a mirror," give the hand signal for sit, then sit. Your dog will sit in response to your hand signal, but she will look like she sat because you sat. Then go on to the next trick. Give her the hand signal for, say, cover your eyes. Then cover your own eyes. She will cover her eyes because you gave her the hand signal, but your audience will think she is copying you. The more hand signals she knows, the more impressive this trick is.

Beyond Tricks

Now that you know how to train your dog, why stop with just tricks? Does your dog bark all day long? Does she pull you like a kite down the street? Does she destroy your stuff when she's left alone?

What do you usually do when she's bad? Do you spank and scold her? Remember that punishment is not usually the best way to teach your dog. If you've punished her once and it didn't work, and you've punished her again and it didn't work, what makes you think that punishing her again and again will work? Why not try to use rewards to get her to do what you want? If she barks too much, you can train her to be quiet. Think of being quiet as a trick. How would you gradually click and reward her for being quiet for longer and longer times?

Sometimes the best way to train your dog not to do something is to train her to do something else she can't do at the same time. This is called *training an incompatible behavior*. For instance, if you want to train her to not jump up on people, train her to sit

DOG HEALTH NOTE

Sometimes a dog that is misbehaving badly or acting in a way she didn't used to act is sick. Her doctor may be able to find out why.

and stay and offer a paw for a reward. When she's doing that trick she can't jump up.

Here are some common behavior problems and ways you can train your dog to behave better.

Barking

If your dog barks at everything, you need to teach her to quiet down when asked. Start when your dog is only slightly likely to bark. Click and reward her for being quiet. Require her to be quiet for gradually longer periods of time—at first just a few seconds, later maybe a minute. When she has mastered that behavior, add a cue: "Quiet!"

and reward her for being quiet after you say it. Gradually move to situations where she is more and more likely to bark, clicking and rewarding her for being quiet for up to a minute in each situation. Don't move to a harder situation until she has mastered an easier one. Your dog won't learn to never bark. She's a dog, and barking is natural. But she should learn to quiet down when you ask her to.

Pulling

If your dog pulls you down the street when you try to walk her, you need to teach her to walk nicely when asked. Start at home away from places that make her pull. Put her on a leash and walk around your house or yard. When she is walking nicely beside you, click and reward her. When she pulls, make her turn around and go away from what she was pulling toward. When she walks nicely again, click and reward her, either with a treat or by letting her go sniff what she was pulling to sniff. After she is walking nicely by your side, introduce a cue word, such as "Heel!" Gradually start walking her to places where she is more likely to pull. Always make

her walk away from what she is pulling toward, and then reward her for walking nicely by letting her go to whatever she was pulling toward. Give her treats for walking nicely by your side.

Digging

Dogs like to dig. The problem is that they usually dig when you're not around, so it's hard to train them not to. It's easier to train them to dig in one place, like a doggy sandbox, where digging is allowed. See if you can make a sandbox for your dog. Bury treats and toys in it so she will want to dig there. Be sure you don't bury anything she can swallow. Keep burying new things for her to find every day. Make her sandbox more fun than the rest of the yard!

Jumping up

Dogs that jump up on people can knock them down or ruin their clothes. The best way to keep your dog from jumping on people is to have her do a trick instead. It can be any trick as long as doing it will make it impossible for her to jump up at the same time. For example, you could have her sit when company comes over. Click and reward her for sitting calmly. But do give her a chance to say hello to your guest. Have your guest kneel down and greet your dog. If your dog still can't be calm, have her lie down and stay. Keep rewarding her for staying still.

Hyperactivity

If your dog is too active, the best thing to do is to tire her out with lots of exercise and lots of training. Then teach her the Be Still trick. You can click and reward her for going to a special bed or a place in a corner of the room. You can give her a special toy that you can stuff with dog treats that will occupy her for a long time. Gradually have her stay longer before rewarding her with a big treat. But don't make her stay there forever!

Destroying

Dogs that destroy things can be harder to help. Puppies tend to chew things up because they don't know any better. The best training to fix this problem is to train you to keep everything out of her reach! Other dogs may destroy things because

they are bored or have too much energy. Taking them for a long walk or run, plus teaching them lots of tricks, will help tire them out. Some other dogs destroy things when they are left alone, because they are afraid of being alone. You have to teach these dogs that being alone isn't scary. You teach them by leaving them just for a few seconds at first, and clicking and rewarding them for being good while you were gone. Practice leaving your dog for short time periods lots of times throughout the day. Work up to longer and longer times, but do it very, very gradually. If she isn't getting any better, your veterinarian may be able to give her something to calm her down to make training go better.

Going to the bathroom inside

If your dog is a puppy, remember she can't go very long without having a bathroom break. You need to make sure she never has a chance to relieve herself inside by taking her out when she wakes up, after she eats, after she plays, and every couple of hours. Have her sleep in a crate—dogs don't want to relieve themselves in their beds—and don't let her have the run of the house. When she relieves herself outside, be sure to click and treat just like you would any other trick. When she relieves herself inside, try to whisk her outside as fast as you can. If you find out later that she's relieved herself inside, it's too late to do anything. Punishing her then won't help. If your dog is an adult, she should get a medical exam to make sure she's not having accidents because she's sick. If she is well, she should be trained the same way you would train a puppy.

Fearfulness

Dogs can be afraid because they don't know what to expect or because they've had bad experiences. The best way to train them not to be afraid is to teach them gradually just like you would teach a trick. The trick is being brave. So you never push your dog into a really scary situation. You just little by little get her used to what she is afraid of, and then reward her for being brave. It helps if you can have her do another trick at the same time so it distracts her and gives you something to reward.

For example, if your dog is afraid of the vacuum cleaner, you may have to turn the vacuum on in the other room. Walk toward it and as soon as your dog seems scared stop right there. Have her do a trick and give her a treat for doing it. Then do another trick. Do not force her to go any closer! Only when she is calm should you take a step closer and do some more tricks. The secret is to never get her so close that she can't get over being scared before you quit that day. You have to be very patient. It may take days or weeks to get her so she isn't afraid of something, and sometimes even then she never will get over her fear.

Biting

Gentle training can sometimes help make mean dogs into friendly dogs. However, this is a job for an adult—or better yet, a dog behavior specialist.

What's Next?

Have you enjoyed training your dog? You can think of lots more tricks on your own. Remember that you can catch funny behaviors if you click and reward them when your dog does them on his own, or you can gradually encourage behaviors your dog doesn't naturally do.

Maybe your dog knows enough tricks to enter a talent contest. Maybe he could entertain at children's hospitals or homes for the elderly. He may need to be certified as a therapy dog so he can visit in hospitals and nursing homes. Maybe he has a future as an animal actor. Several animal actor agencies keep information about talented dogs in their files in case they are needed for a project.

Maybe you would like to make a career out of animal training. You could train dogs to be actors, guide dogs, animal assistants, therapy dogs, obedience competitors, or just good companions. You could train dolphins at marine parks, wild animals at zoos, or all sorts of animal actors. You could go to college and take classes in animal learning and animal behavior. You might want to become a veterinarian and specialize in helping animals with behavior problems. You might want to become a psychologist and help people—remember how the same training techniques worked with people as they did with dogs?

Chances are, though, that you just want to be the best friend you can be to your dog. And that's a pretty good trick right there.

Index